Write. Open. Act.

An Intentional Life Planning Workbook

Lee Weinstein

Intentional Life Planning, LLC

Write, Open, Act: An Intentional Life Planning Workbook

ISBN 978-0-9994118-0-3

INTENTIONAL LIFE PLANNING, LLC
Portland, Oregon, USA
writeopenact.com
info@writeopenact.com

Written by Lee Weinstein
Edited by Andrea Carlos
Designed by DiDi Davidovich
Illustrated by Clare Davidovich
Book production by Jain Lemos

Based on an Intentional Life Planning process and workshop originated by
Lee and Melinda Weinstein.

For Melinda, Mel, Emma and Sophie

"REMEMBERING THAT I'LL BE DEAD SOON
IS THE MOST IMPORTANT TOOL I'VE EVER
ENCOUNTERED TO HELP ME MAKE THE BIG
CHOICES IN LIFE. BECAUSE ALMOST
EVERYTHING — ALL EXTERNAL EXPECTATIONS,
ALL PRIDE, ALL FEAR OF EMBARRASSMENT OR
FAILURE — THESE THINGS JUST FALL AWAY
IN THE FACE OF DEATH, LEAVING ONLY WHAT
IS TRULY IMPORTANT. REMEMBERING THAT
YOU ARE GOING TO DIE IS THE BEST WAY I
KNOW TO AVOID THE TRAP OF THINKING YOU
HAVE SOMETHING TO LOSE. YOU ARE ALREADY
NAKED. THERE IS NO REASON NOT TO FOLLOW
YOUR HEART..."

—**Steve Jobs,** *Apple Inc. co-founder*
Stanford University Commencement Address, 2005

Contents

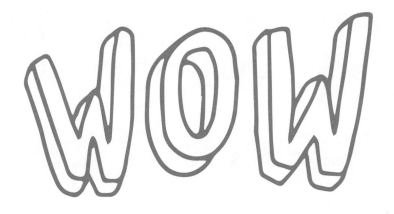

"THIS IS OUR LIFE HAPPENING...
AND IT'S HAPPENING RIGHT NOW."

—Michael Chabon

Praise for 'Write, Open, Act'

"It's tempting to say this life-planning process changed my life, but that would sound hyperbolic. Instead, I will say that thanks to it, I have been able to accomplish some very big things in the last 18 months of my life that I had procrastinated for over a decade. These include doing a concert/fundraiser for my friends and family and launching a new nonprofit organization."

—**Ashley Henry,** *chief collaboration officer, Business for a Better Portland*

"A moment of true clarity arrives when you step back and see both your and your partner's goals, desires and wishes clearly laid out against the years ahead. You realize you can aspire to achieve a little more, to shorten that list of dreams deferred."

—**Jason Davis,** *owner, Merge Design*

"Even if you don't do everything in this workbook, you will still be impacted. And Sticky Notes are really old school but it works!"

—**Dr. Maile O'Hara,** *Ph.D. M.Ed., clinical psychologist*

"Is this life-changing? Yes, absolutely. The process is as valuable and as fun as the end product. You start your ILP journey by calculating how much time you have left on earth. Once you've reaffirmed that every minute counts, you get to figure out how you'll fill those minutes with adventure, fun and even the mundane. You emerge with a road map that shows you how to take the life you have and make it the life you want. Super cool!"

—**Steve Shropshire,** *attorney at law, Jordan Ramis PC*

"Answering the thought-provoking life-planning questions and then putting my goals on a timeline helped me get much clearer about my life goals—in particular, a memoir I want to write before I die. My memoir is no longer just some pie-in-the-sky idea, but a solid plan with concrete deadlines I am working toward every month."

—**Andrea Carlos,** *Carlos Communications*

"SAY WHAT YOU THINK. LOVE WHO YOU LOVE. 'CAUSE
YOU JUST GET SO MANY TRIPS AROUND THE SUN. JUST
FOLLOW YOUR ARROW, WHEREVER IT POINTS."

—Kacey Musgraves, *"Follow Your Arrow"*

Introduction

One Saturday, my wife, Melinda, and I pulled out a large sheet of butcher paper and invented a process we call "Intentional Life Planning."

It began with a conversation about where we wanted to live, and led to our looking at the decades we had ahead and the key upcoming milestones for our family, and imagining what we wanted to do with our lives.

We ended up creating a highly visual Intentional Life Plan—a timeline filled with dreams and goals—that we have updated every year since.

Then one year we shared photos of our annual planning day on Facebook, and our friends went crazy. Many asked how they, too, could get started. And several asked us to turn our process into a workshop and a book. I was stunned by how many didn't have a plan or a process. Our friend Tracy commented, "This is amazing! I am so inspired to do this with my husband. This is the smartest thing ever! How do we start?" Nicole responded, "Agreed, it is the smartest thing, ever. Why wouldn't we apply strategic planning to our personal and holistic lives as we do in our professional lives?"

After our friends asked for our guidance to help them plan their lives, we started conducting Intentional Life Planning workshops for individuals and couples in 2014. We have held several workshops across Oregon, and those participants now have Intentional Life Plans at home, many hanging on hallway walls and stairwells as visual reminders of their life goals.

"Write, Open, Act" is meant to bring the Intentional Life Planning method to a wider audience to explore on their own. *Writing* down your life's wishes *opens* up new possibilities that you can *act* on to live a fulfilling life. Our hope is that this workbook helps everyone plan for and lead their best life.

This workbook is about doing and hands-on planning and not a lot of reading. You can build your Intentional Life Plan in half a day, and we'll give you the tools to implement your plan.

So, go make your life happen! After all, "You just get so many trips around the sun."

Warmly,

Lee

Why Create an Intentional Life Plan?

Life goes by fast. And the older we get, the more quickly time seems to go: One day, you're fresh out of school. The next, you're onto your third job, or having your first child, or suddenly attending your 35th college reunion.

Where did time go? Are you living a life intended and getting done what you want?

A lot of people want to take life as it comes each day. They don't plan, and they just want to "live life." Many can't—or won't—plan beyond the next 24 hours. That may be out of necessity, philosophy or lifestyle. But living your life passively may not add up to a life well-lived. In fact, you may realize that life has passed you by and moved on without you.

Two years ago, we took my father back to his birthplace—and he couldn't believe it had been 25 years since his last visit. He hadn't seen his relatives there or the home where he grew up in eons. It was a wonderful visit, but tinged with a slight melancholy for what had been missed.

That's the purpose of this workbook: to help you plan your best life and to use your time here on this planet the way you intended it.

I've always been a planner, and heading public relations at Nike for 15 years, we had to plan for everything—a shoe launch, a sporting event or a company announcement. Our plans included goals, strategies, actions, timelines and measures.

If life were a project like the kind you're asked to complete at work or school, and you knew you had a limited time to get it done, wouldn't it make sense to develop a plan? You only have a certain amount of time to live this life: What do you want to get done—and when will you get started? What would its successful achievement look like?

The insight for this book came when Melinda and I were discussing where we wanted to live. I was 41 and she was 36, and it was clear we had another 40 or 50 years left to live. Suddenly we realized we could—and we should—plan our moves. We stretched 12 feet of butcher paper across our kitchen counter and started with a timeline across the top, charting out each year from 2001 to 2041. We then added our major life milestones—when we'd be 50, 60, 70, etc. We included the years our children would start driving, graduate from high school and college, and set out on interesting paths of their own. We wrote down when we might have grandchildren. And we added when our parents would be older and require more support from us.

We divided the timeline into decades, and suddenly 40 years became a much smaller unit—just four decades—and we saw even more clearly the need to use that time intentionally and with purpose. We created heaps of Sticky Notes with goals including:

- Find a new job
- Start a business
- Sell house
- Buy a farm
- Run a 5K
- Visit Yellowstone National Park
- Go to Montana
- Take daughters to Italy
- Develop investment plan
- Support Mom and Dad
- Sell business
- Move to Hawaii

We've updated our Intentional Life Plan every year since and have developed an effective process to stay focused on our life goals, assessing and updating our plans both monthly and annually—a process that we'll share with you.

It's amazing to go back and see we've accomplished 90 percent of what we wrote in our first Intentional Life Plan!

By way of background, my parents were divorced, and I grew up with a single mother who worked at a Nordstrom cosmetics counter when I was in high school. I got my first taste of employment as a busboy at age 13. I graduated with a political science degree from Lewis & Clark College, and worked in political communications for a congressman, governor and AIDS agency before joining Nike, where I directed communications for 15 years. Melinda is the daughter of a public high school choir teacher father and a mother who worked in retail sales, and is a high school graduate who has worked her entire adult life. She served as an administrative assistant at Nike for 20 years and is a fantastic stepmother of two. We both left Nike and started a PR agency, which we have co-owned since 2007.

What Intentional Life Planning workshop participants said about this process:

"Great to get out all my rambling ideas and put them on paper."

—Graduate student

"This helped me understand how much I knew I wanted but wasn't aware of."

—Nonprofit consultant

"The visual representation of our life plan on paper really works."

—Freelance writer

"Before starting this, I had a loose idea of the direction I wanted to go with my work. As I wrote on the timeline, new goals/visions came forward that I had no idea were there."

—Realtor

"The visual tool of the timeline is great! As well as the reminder to revisit, because life is finite."

—City planner

"Great process to be introspective on both an individual and couples level, and then to convert those thoughts into action."

—Doctor

Boxes throughout this workbook contain quotations, thoughts and advice from our Intentional Life Planning workshop participants and friends.

How to Use This Workbook

This is a practical four-step workbook that will help you discover your life's dreams and goals, ultimately living your life with intention and a plan.

· It's important for you to do all the legwork *before* your Intentional Life Planning Day.

· Complete each of the four steps in the order they appear.

The exercises in this workbook are essential for those of you who want to live life fully—knowing that life is finite, filled with change and twists and turns, but that with a plan and a steady view toward the horizon, you can accomplish most, if not all, of your life's goals.

Once you've completed your timeline, we want you to hang it someplace where you can occasionally stop and look at it. We humans are visual, and there is great power in having a large, visual timeline on paper. You can see and remember what you have envisioned, ask yourself what progress you're making, and smile and celebrate your achievements—adjusting your plan as life moves forward and your goals change.

Yes, life happens, but if you *write down* a visual Intentional Life Plan, you can create a framework to live your life by. Then, with action steps and deadlines, you can and will make your life happen.

The bottom line is that an Intentional Life Plan is the map to keep your life on course—your arrow to a life well-lived.

This workbook will change your life. At the end, you'll have:

· **A clear view of your life's wishes and goals**

· **A visual Intentional Life Plan and timeline**

· **Steps to help you realize your plan**

· **Tools to manage your plan**

· **Resources to help you along the way**

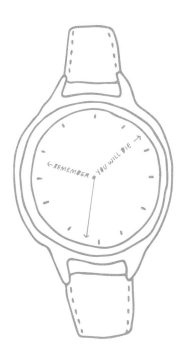

You don't want to be lying on your deathbed wishing you'd gone to Italy, or told your dad you loved him. You want, at the end, to say you lived your life well, and spent your time traveling around the sun with intention.

So, let's get planning!

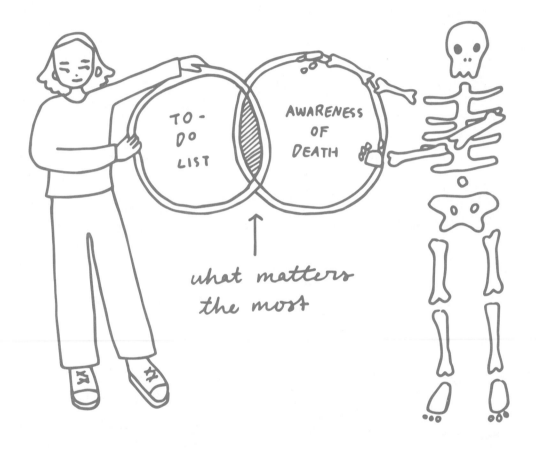

TO-
DO
LIST

AWARENESS
OF
DEATH

↑
*what matters
the most*

GLOSSARY

Intentional Life Plan	A visual plan and timeline of your intended life goals, including key milestones that you can adjust as life moves forward.
Intentional Life Planning Day	A day you will set aside at least once a year to create or update your Intentional Life Plan.
Life Goals	The 1 to 10 significant things you want to achieve each year.
Action Steps	A series of specific, concrete steps that make a life goal easy to achieve.

Which day(s) will you set aside each year as your Intentional Life Planning Day?

....

....

....

....

....

....

Uncover Your Life's Wishes

In Step 1 you'll get:

1. Questions and advice to help identify your life's wishes

2. A clear understanding of where your life is and where you're going

3. The preparation you need to put your life plan into action

Start by Digging

Step 1 in developing your Intentional Life Plan is to take time to do some digging and get your blood—and ideas—flowing. Reach into your soul and back to your childhood dreams.

As the great poet Rainer Maria Rilke wrote in "Letters to a Young Poet," solitude is key to finding your path: "Solitude will be a support and a home for you, even in the midst of very unfamiliar circumstances, and from it you will find all your paths. ... If you will stay close to nature, to its simplicity, to the small things hardly noticeable, those things can unexpectedly become great and immeasurable."

I fundamentally believe all our true answers lie within our soul. It's great having friends and advisers to talk with, but why would you live the life someone else asked you to live? When it comes down to it, this is your life and your truth, and you just have to access that truth, pay attention to it always and live it with intention.

You've had thoughts racing around your head, coming to you in the shower, and things you've been asking yourself for years. Sometimes we also get so busy "doing"—or spending time on our screens—that we don't take time to just sit and be.

I hiked all over northern Oregon on the weekends, as part of a series of things I did to access my soul and spend time with just me to see what came up as I pondered leaving Nike and our future life. As I walked, thoughts percolated. I dictated notes along the way, and through that process discovered all sorts of things that I'd been thinking about but hadn't noticed or paid any attention.

"CARL JUNG, THE FAMOUS SWISS PSYCHIATRIST, COINED THE TERM 'SYNCHRONICITY' TO DESCRIBE THE COMING TOGETHER OF INNER AND OUTER EVENTS IN WAYS THAT ARE MEANINGFUL TO THE OBSERVER BUT CANNOT BE EXPLAINED BY CAUSE AND EFFECT. THE WILDERNESS IS A FERTILE TIME FOR SYNCHRONICITIES BECAUSE, AS JUNG OBSERVED, PERIODS OF EMOTIONAL INTENSITY AND UPHEAVAL OPEN US UP TO PSYCHOLOGICAL BREAKTHROUGHS. SOMETIMES THE MESSAGES THAT COME THROUGH FROM SYNCHRONICITIES ARE NOT IMMEDIATELY CLEAR, BUT GRADUALLY, WE FIND CLARITY. THE KEY IS TO ALLOW THEM TO SHOW UP, TO BE OPEN TO ANYTHING."

—**Ruth Luban**, *"Are You a Corporate Refugee?"*

> *"When I was a little girl, I'd write down my dreams on scraps of paper and throw them in a cookie jar—a ceramic schnauzer whose head lifted off that sat on a shelf in my bedroom. Those dreams were the ones that tended to materialize, so I thought the schnauzer had magical powers. Turns out, it was the pen and paper. I'm with y'all on writing stuff down."*
>
> —Mid-40s mother of two and writer

On a hike up Saddle Mountain on the Oregon Coast, I stopped to meditate along a creek in a mild rain, and I'll never forget watching a drop of water—a beautiful drop of water—fall from one leaf to the next. Taking time is important, listening to the silence, asking and inquiring.

In her book "Are You a Corporate Refugee?" my friend and career counselor Ruth Luban describes this process as "entering The Wilderness. A process of wandering," which can be internal for some people or an external physical exploration for others.

Luban suggests joyful creative play during the wilderness process to access other parts of your mind and soul. I started painting and drawing. She also suggests daily rituals such as keeping a creative journal, mindful eating and developing an exercise ritual.

Take notes along the way as you begin your soulful digging. It may be uncomfortable. You may have conflicting thoughts. You don't know what may come up.

There was a time in my life when I really had no idea what I wanted to do next. I've always been a goal-oriented person, and to suddenly think I didn't have any goals was terrifying. But Luban's process of allowing that to be OK, to go into the wilderness, and to journal daily and meditate, was incredibly valuable. It helped me open my mind.

Let the Creativity and Spontaneity Begin

A month before you schedule your Intentional Life Planning Day (Step 2), take time to complete these exercises. The goal is to get your creative juices and your thoughts and feelings flowing—and to put the universe in motion.

1. ANSWER THESE QUESTIONS

What's your philosophy? What do you view as your purpose here on earth?

....

....

....

....

What's working in your life?

....

....

....

....

What's not working in your life?

....

....

....

....

What makes you happiest?

....

....

....

....

How do you view aging? How do you view staying young?

....

....

....

....

What do you lack that you think you still need?

....

....

....

....

What fascinated you as a kid, and what did you dream about being and doing as an adult?

....

....

....

....

Where do you want to wake up 5, 10, 15, 20 years from now?

....

....

....

....

What's left undone in your life?

....

....

....

....

....

....

....

What are your biggest accomplishments?

....

....

....

....

....

What else do you want to accomplish by the time you die?

....

....

....

....

What is your definition of a successful life?

....

....

....

....

Where were the turning points in your life, and what hopes and dreams did you leave behind at those forks in the road?

....

....

....

....

What do you love doing now (personal/fun/work)?

....

....

....

....

....

What do you want the next step of your life to be about?

....

....

....

....

....

....

....

2. DO FURTHER DIGGING

Here are some trigger questions to get you thinking. You can also use Sticky Notes to create goals based on your answers to these questions.

Bring your ideas with you to your Intentional Life Planning Day.

Happiness

- How happy or satisfied are you?
- What would make you happier?
- What's making you unhappy?
- Do you want to see a therapist?

Career

- Where are you in your career?
- Are you happy in your current job/profession?
- What do you aspire to be?
- Are you at the level you desire in your job?
- How long do you want to be at your current job?
- When do you see a future career change?
- Would you want to go back to school to add skills/ knowledge?
- What other jobs would you like to do?
- How long do you want to work?
- How long do you need to work?
- Do you want to retire? When?
- Do you want to work in retirement? What's your ideal retirement job?

Finances

- How are you doing financially?
- What are the key issues?
- Do you have a budget? Is it working?
- Are you saving for retirement?
- Do you have a financial plan or planner?
- Do you have other expenses (tuition, long-term care/ disability insurance)?
- What does retirement mean to you? Will you ever truly retire, or will you have a different career?
- How much money do you need/want for later in life?
- When will you retire and start using your retirement funds?
- How's your insurance? Will? Advance directives? Power of attorney?
- What if your partner/ spouse passes/becomes incapacitated?

Home

- Do you like where you live? Do you want to change it?
- When did you last paint, decorate or rearrange the furniture?
- Where else would you like to live?
- Do you dream of living somewhere else?
- Do you want to retire in your current home? If not, where? What about selling everything and traveling or retiring in another country?
- Do you want to live overseas?

Vital & Present

- What's your philosophy of life?
- How are you staying current? Are you reading current literature? Staying up on new technology? Asking young people questions?
- Do you like change?
- Do you look forward to growing older? Retiring?
- Do you want to stay young at heart? If so, what are you going to do about it?
- What do you want to stop/start?
- Do you want or have friends of different backgrounds, races, ages or from different countries?

Family & Traditions

- What's working or not?
- Are there familial repairs needed?
- Are there traditions you want to start or stop? What do you do around spring break, summer, major holidays and religious observances?
- What does your family do together each year?
- As your children get older, what traditions do you all want to have? Have you discussed this together?
- Will there be grandkids? Where will they live? Where will you live?

Parents & Grandparents

- How are your parents/grandparents?
- What are you doing to stay in touch with them?
- Do you tell them you love them each time you talk?
- What special rituals do you have with them?
- Should you have breakfast with your mom, dad, grandfather or grandmother separately each month?
- Do you call them daily, weekly or monthly?
- What are their end-of-life wishes?
- Do you know who their doctors are? Insurers? Where their vital records are? Passwords?
- Have you asked them about your family history? Do you have a family tree? Do you want to record them talking about their lives or your family history?
- Are all those family photos digitized? Do you know who's in all the photos, or should they help you catalog them?
- How will you plan to manage your grief and their affairs after their passing?

Community

- Are you involved in your community?
- Do you want to do more or less in your community/ neighborhood?
- Are you giving back? Are you a giver as well as a taker?
- Are there things you want to learn or people you want to meet?
- What's your responsibility to your community, neighborhood or school?
- Do you want to mentor a child or take on a foster child?
- Are you helping the next generation?
- Are you leaving the world better than you found it?

Learning

- What else do you want to learn?
- What are you curious about?
- Do you want to go (back) to college?
- Do you want to take a class?
- How are you keeping your mind agile?
- What was the last class you took?
- What weird/unusual thing have you always been curious about?

Creativity

- How are you being creative?
- What are you doing to nurture your creative side?
- Do you want to do something new or different around your creative side? Pick up the guitar again? Fire up that old kiln? Take a painting class? Start scrapbooking?
- Do you listen to music?
- Do you go to performances?
- What museums have you always wanted to go to?

Sex & Mates

- How's your sex life?
- Do you have sex often enough?
- Are there areas you want to explore?
- Are there things you want to change?
- Are you a good mate?

Spiritual

- How's your spiritual life?
- What would you like to explore?
- Do you belong to an organized religion? If so, do you want to do more or less around it? If you aren't currently a member, do you want to become one?
- What are you doing to nurture your spiritual journey (meditation, groups, being in nature, lectures)?
- Are you doing enough for your spiritual self?

Health, Wellness & Recreation

- How's your health?
- What do you need to do about it?
- Are you still attractive to your mate?
- When was your last physical? Mammogram? PSA test? Eye or dental exam?
- Are you exercising four to six times a week? Do you want a physical trainer?
- Are you moving enough? Do you move every hour?
- How are your muscles?
- Do you get regular aerobic exercise?
- How's your cholesterol?
- How are you managing stress? Work/life balance?
- Do you turn off the screens and email alerts?
- When was the last time you walked? Lain in the grass and watched the clouds? Read a book or magazine?

Diet

- How's your eating?
- How much meat are you eating compared to vegetables and fruits?
- Do you have an eating system you stick to?
- Do you need to eat more, less or better?
- Do you want to become a vegetarian or vegan?
- What about seeing a dietitian for advice?

Project & Hobbies

- Are there special projects you want or need to do?
- Are there new hobbies you want to learn?
- What about that addition to the house or the landscaping you always wanted to do?

Clutter

- How much clutter do you have in your life?
- Are there possessions you can get rid of?
- Do you need it if you haven't used it in the last six months or year?
- Can you digitize it and get rid of it?
- Will you be leaving your descendants a big fat mess, or can you purge it now?

Social & Friendships

- Who are your best friends?
- As a couple, who are your best friends or best couples?
- Whom do you want to see and how often?
- Are there important friends you want to have regular contact with or do special things with?
- When was the last time you made a new friend?
- Are you a good friend?
- How will you acquire new friends?
- Are there social activities you'd like to do (poker, mahjong, golf, bridge)?

Travel

- Where have you always wanted to go?
- Where do you still have left to visit?
- Have you been to every national park? Top of the Sydney Harbour Bridge? Do you want to?
- Do you need to travel?

Habits

- What habits do you want to break?
- How's your alcohol consumption? Tobacco use? Nails and biting?
- What new habits do you want to start?
- What do you want to do daily, weekly, monthly, yearly?

Getting Older

- As you get older, what do you want to do or not do?
- Where do you want to live and how?
- If you got diagnosed with a debilitating or degenerative disease (Alzheimer's, ALS, Parkinson's), what would your wishes be?
- Assisted living? Nursing homes? Senior living arrangements?

Emergencies & Obstacles

- Are you prepared for an earthquake, tsunami, fire or other natural disasters?
- Do your kids know where to meet you if electronics fail?
- If your partner died today, do you have your plans/papers in order?

End-of-Life

- How do you want your life to end? Where?

- Do you have an end-of-life plan including your wishes for care? Is it legally documented?

- How do you want to be remembered?

- Do you want to have an end-of-life celebration before you die?

- Are your end-of-life wishes known to your loved one(s)?

- If you had six months left to live, what would you do?

- What do you want to leave behind? Do you want to support a cause? Be memorialized in some way? Support your alma mater or favorite charity?

3. WRITE YOUR OBITUARY

How do you want your obituary—your story—to read when you die?

This is an excellent and sobering exercise. It's useful to check in on where you are on your life's journey, how you want to live your life and what you value, and what you still have to accomplish.

Take a morning and have your resume or LinkedIn profile nearby for reference. Think about how you want your obituary to sound (your tone/philosophy/life outlook). You might check out a few obituaries online.

"Mary Ellen (Lowe) Monson, 95, passed away Dec. 29, 2015. Mary Ellen loved a drink and a sad song, preferably together and especially with friends and family. She enjoyed a lifetime of TV (a perk of not having a job), never drove (with a license), did not answer the phone during 'Jeopardy' and grieved Regis Philbin's retirement daily. She loved her grandchildren, though liked them best when they were young enough to stay on her lap and old enough to run to the liquor store. Mary Ellen always wanted her obituary to say that she was an avid reader because she thought those people sounded smart. Mary Ellen was an avid reader."

—**The Oregonian**, *May 11-15, 2016*

Start with your full name, age, date of birth and date of death. ....

....

Where was your last residence? ....

....

How did you die? (How would you like to die?)

Where did you grow up? Where else did you live?

Did you marry? Whom and where?

Did you serve in the military?

Where did you attend school?

What awards or accolades did you win?

What brought you your greatest joy?

What was your greatest disappointment?

What favorite stories do you want people to remember about you? Humor?

....

What did you like to do? What hobbies did you have? What did you believe in?

....

Where did you work?

....

What did you achieve outside of work?

....

What did you believe in?

....

What volunteer activities did you do?

....

Who were your parents, siblings and spouses? Who are you survived by? Pets?

....

Will you have a memorial service? If so, where/what? Public or private?

....

What do you want done with your body? ....

....

Do you want people to make donations in your memory? Where? ....

....

Do you have any favorite quotations? ....

....

What three to five words describe how you lived? ....

....

4. SUMMARIZE YOUR OBITUARY

....

....

....

....

....

....

"WE ARE ONLY HERE FOR A MINUTE, WE ARE HERE FOR A LITTLE WINDOW, AND TO USE THAT TIME TO CATCH AND SHARE SHARDS OF LIGHT AND LAUGHTER AND GRACE SEEMS TO ME THE GREAT STORY."

—Brian Doyle

5. REVIEW WHAT YOU'VE LEARNED

Once you've answered the questions and written your obituary, go back and review your responses:

- · What resonated with you?

- · What was new that you hadn't heard or considered before?

- · Where were their similarities and divergences?

- · What excited you?

- · What scared you?

I'll never forget doing digging exercises in the midst of a career transition and remembering that as a sixth-grader I wrote and sold door-to-door a neighborhood newspaper, and dreamed of having a camper and traveling the U.S. writing about the people along the way. It confirmed to me that I'd always had communications in my blood!

Things that resonate are confirming, but pay attention to any funny feelings or questions you may want to mull further. There may be good reasons for being scared, or you may want to look behind the anxiety and what the root cause or blockage might be.

This digging is solely for you—it's up to you if and how you share with friends or partners.

6. GIVE YOUR WORK TIME TO SINK IN

Critically, let this work gel after it's done. Thoughts and feelings may come up afterward. Pay attention to them and, if you want, go back and make additional notes. The gelling process is really important and seeps into your soul. Pay attention to thoughts as you shower, drive or work out.

Bring this work with you to your Intentional Life Planning Day so you can refer to it as you build your Intentional Life Plan.

Tips for Unlocking Your Life's Dreams

Many people don't know what they want from life, especially young people and retirees. Some people aren't goal-oriented. Others may be less linear and more circular in their thinking. Others may be more spiritual in their approach.

It's OK if you don't know exactly what you want from life or you get stuck. Allow yourself that permission. Recognize if you're not sure, and take a deep breath. If you encounter roadblocks as you start digging, take a step back and test some other ways to access your desires and passions.

"DO NOT COMPLAIN. WORK HARDER. SPEND MORE TIME ALONE."

—Joan Didion

Here are several tips for reaching into your soul to uncover your life's dreams:

- **Start a meditation practice.** Go into the "wilderness" and allow yourself to be. Set aside 10 to 20 minutes first thing every morning to sit, be and breathe. There are lots of books, classes, apps and YouTube videos to teach you how to meditate. I find meditation essential, and it also feels to me like a gateway to the universe.

- **Write your stream-of-consciousness thoughts.** In her seminal book, "The Artist's Way," Julia Cameron suggests writing "Morning Pages"—three pages of longhand, stream-of-consciousness writing, done first thing in the morning—to record anything and everything that crosses your mind. The process of writing longhand slows down the brain and opens up creativity. Not editing as you go is essential—just get it out there. Allow your synapses to fire and your thinking to open.

- **Create lists.** Lists can be valuable for lots of people. The key is to be able to find them! Create a folder and throw your ideas and notes in it. Go back and bucket those notes into lists by type (future jobs, travel, finances). Keep those in the folder, or consider putting them on your computer. I use Evernote, a note-taking application that syncs across computers, smartphones and tablets, and have several ongoing lists I can immediately find there. I also use Day One, a journaling app, and have a separate journal with my "Next Career" thoughts.

- **Spend time alone.** I find nature to be a great place to open my mind: hiking, sitting and pondering, skinny-dipping, walking along the beach by myself.

- **Take a class or read something different.** Classes and doing very different thinking can also stimulate ideas and action. Take a design or poetry class. Study or read about something completely different from what you do day-to-day. Look at art.

- **See a therapist.** Working with a therapist one-on-one or in a group can also be extremely useful. Talking out loud with a professional who can guide you or in a safe group where you can voice your thinking and receive feedback can help you discover what's important.

Remember to Dream

My friend Megan designed a "dream cloud" to inspire her to consider her professional future. She wrote down six big dreams, and then explained the significance of each.

"I did this dream cloud as part of another workbook called 'The Fire Starter Sessions' by Danielle LaPorte," Megan recounts. "This entire series of exercises was designed to help me explore and find my natural strengths—the things I do well without expelling excess energy. My hope was to increase awareness around these areas and apply them in my professional life. What I learned is that I'm passionate about helping others; working with a strong, dedicated team and being creative is a must for me in any job or role I desire."

She continues: "The beauty about this exercise is that it gave me permission to let my mind wander without boundaries or barriers. I wrote freely as things popped into my head. As my dreams continue to change and take new shape I'll plan to do this again, especially if or when I'm looking to make another shift professionally or personally."

Megan's work also serves as a reminder to dream as you're doing this planning and when you're out and about—and to take notes about those dreams. Dreaming serves a purpose at work also: Sometimes we jump immediately into our work plans and to-do lists, and we don't take time to dream about crazy ideas, what amazing success would look like, or how we might thrill our customers or patrons.

DEVELOP A
LEADERSHIP/TEACHING
PROGRAM FOR FITNESS
PROFESSIONALS

I WANT THIS BECAUSE...
HAVING LEARNED SO MANY SKILLS I
WOULD LIKE TO SHARE WITH OTHERS

PRODUCING
DANCE VIDEOS
THAT TELL
A STORY

OWN AND
RUN MY OWN
DANCE COMPANY

I WANT THIS BECAUSE...
I WANT TO CREATE A PLACE FOR
PEOPLE LIKE ME WANTING TO
LEARN AND CREATE

DREAMS

I WANT THIS
BECAUSE...
CONNECTING W/ MY CREATIVE
ENERGY THROUGH DANCE AND
STORYTELLING PUSHING ME TO
BE A BETTER CHOREOGRAPHER

WRITE A BOOK
ON MY LIFE
JOURNEY

I WANT THIS
BECAUSE...
I AM PASSIONATE AND
INSPIRED BY HEALTH,
WELLNESS, ATHLETICISM
AND WOMEN

MASTER THE ART OF
BRANDING ⅓ LOGO
DESIGN

WORK FOR NIKE
IN THE WOMEN'S
FITNESS DEPT.

"REMEMBER, WE'RE ALL IN THIS ALONE."

—Lily Tomlin

Special Instructions for Couples in Step 1

It's your life. What you do with it, what values you live and what you seek to accomplish are up to you. As Dr. Harville Hendrix, author of "Getting the Love You Want," puts it, "Marriage, ultimately, is the practice of being passionate friends. The two individuals in a relationship need to let go of the illusion that they are the center of the universe and learn to see each other as equal partners. There are indeed two people in the relationship."

Both of you have a right to achieve your own individual life's goals and wishes. As passionate friends, you can help each other achieve your dreams. At times, you may need to go your separate ways. For example, your partner may not be interested in climbing the Seven Summits of the world.

That being said, this work can be highly emotional for couples. It may feel unsafe or threatening. We've had couples in our workshops who could not do this work together on their own and needed a workshop structure and guide.

Complete the exercises in Step 1 by yourself. Then schedule a time for you and your partner to sit down and talk about what came up for you.

- Let one person share first and the other be the receiver.
- Do not judge the other person's thinking, ideas or goals. You are not critics—you are passionate friends!
- Listen, take notes and thank your partner for sharing.
- Afterward, switch sharer/receiver roles and repeat the process above.

Let this gel. Don't react. Consider. Keep your notes and come back to them on your Intentional Life Planning Day. If this brings up major issues, consider working with a therapist. Imago Relationship Therapy is the best relationship work I know, invented by Dr. Hendrix and his wife, Dr. Helen LaKelly Hunt. Consider an Imago workshop or therapist (imagorelationships.org), or another therapist or spiritual adviser.

Special Instructions for People 60+

For those of you 60+ who have done so much in life and who have less time left, Intentional Life Planning is just as important, if not more. Why?

1. THE NOTION OF "RETIREMENT" IS CHANGING

Yes, some people have saved well and are retiring in the conventional sense of the term. Others are seeing this as a time of change and an opportunity to start different or part-time work, and to explore new creative pursuits. Many may not be able to retire because they can't afford to, don't have pensions or haven't saved enough money, or have an infirm loved one.

My grandfather was forced by his company to retire at 65, and it literally killed him. He loved working and the social interactions it entailed. He and his wife didn't like suddenly being together all the time. There was no plan. He lived only another 11 years. On the other hand, my friend Dr. Sally Kaufmann, a Jungian psychiatrist, is now 82 and continues to see patients, albeit part-time. My friend Pete, formerly a general physician, now works part-time as a portrait photographer. My friend Janice Druian studied for her masters in fine arts and went on to a long career in human resources. Upon retirement, she began studying oil painting and re-established herself as an artist; she now shows in galleries, has had three museum shows and was featured in *The Artist's Magazine*. Her husband, Greg, moonlighted as a jazz guitarist in graduate school and went on to an information technology career. He's retired and now has professional gigs playing jazz guitar. "We're both fulfilling our passions," exclaims Janice.

Personally, I don't buy the societal myth that 60+ is a time to start the downward spiral to the end of life. Our society is ageist, and we need to fight against this prejudice. I see 60+ as a time of possibility. Of learning. Of teaching. Of challenging myself to stay young. A time to stay on top of pop culture. Great literature. New technology.

I've pondered "retirement" (I hate this word), and my wife says I'll last about a week before I run out of things to do (and no doubt drive her crazy). Because of this, I may work full- or part-time into my 80s and 90s. So I'm pondering second businesses, mentoring kids or becoming a hotel concierge in Hawaii. My plan is in the works!

2. WE'RE LIVING LONGER, WHICH REQUIRES DIFFERENT PLANNING

We used to plan to live until we're 78. Then it became mid-80s. Now, more and more people are living into their 90s. It's amazing!

That means we may need to work longer to live longer. We may want to consider a "retirement job" that helps supplement our savings and Social Security. Let's face it, retirement is expensive: As Maurie Backman writes on The Motley Fool website, "While Social Security can help cover some of your expenses, your benefits will only suffice in replacing roughly 40 percent of your pre-retirement income. Most seniors, however, need a minimum of 80 percent of their former earnings to pay the bills, especially when you factor long-term care into the mix."

Many people are considering "pre-tirement"—a middle state between being employed and being retired—where they work half- or three-quarters time, do something completely different career-wise at times, or volunteer. I have friends now in their 60s and 70s who no longer have the drive to be at the top of the heap, and they're really enjoying letting that go and savoring their new time and freedom.

Our longer lifespans are also a great gift. As the 2017 HBO documentary "If You're Not in the Obit, Eat Breakfast" points out, many people living into their 90s are today publishing books, running marathons, working out daily, teaching yoga, parachuting from planes and starting new careers. Are you considering you may live a lot longer than 78-85?

In their book "Younger Next Year," Chris Crowley and Henry S. Lodge write about the importance of connections ("There is a grave risk of isolation in America, where we value individualism so highly. And it gets worse in retirement, when we step out of the 'limbic stew' of the workplace. It makes a ton of sense to fight that risk tooth and nail. To make a hard, conscious effort to make new connections… to stay deeply connected with and caring about family and friends and others, all the way out."); exercise (six days a week!); setting a desperate goal and working like crazy to get there; and nutrition ("'QUIT EATING CRAP!' Excellent advice in a country where powerful forces are hard at work, around the clock, trying to persuade you to do just the opposite."). There's now a series of related books and a website: youngernextyear.com. How will you add these four elements to your plan and lifestyle?

"IT IS NOT TRUE THAT PEOPLE STOP PURSUING DREAMS BECAUSE THEY GROW OLD, THEY GROW OLD BECAUSE THEY STOP PURSUING DREAMS."

—Gabriel García Márquez

3. WE'RE ENTERING OUR THIRD ACT (NOT OUR FOURTH)

In her book "Prime Time," Jane Fonda writes about 60+ as her Third Act, which "can allow us to discover who we really are. Entered with intention, Third Acts allow us a second adult lifetime." She sees age as potential—for wisdom, authenticity and wholeness. She suggests planning our Third Act by doing a "life review" of our first two acts—Act I (birth-29) when we "gather all the ingredients—the tools, the skills, the scars—that make us uniquely us." Then Act II, ages 30-59, a period of transition and "building in-betweenness."

After you've done your life review, begin looking ahead to 60+ and complete the exercises that follow. By the way, have you noticed how Fonda's career has just taken off since she entered her Third Act? That's the power of writing things down and being intentional!

4. YOUR LIFE'S PURPOSE MAY RISE TO A NEW CHALLENGE

Even if we've had a life's purpose up until 60+, with kids out of college or careers at their zenith, about this time many of us start to wonder what our life's purpose is now. It may be that you want to take care of your grandkids or an ill neighbor up the road, or help rebuild an athletic facility in your community or join a nonprofit board. It could be that you want to run for mayor or president.

Nike co-founder Phil Knight, in his book, "Shoe Dog," writes, "Life is growth. You grow or you die." What do you want your life's purpose to be now? "Purpose is a universal human need. Without it, we feel bereft of meaning and happiness," writes Joseph P. Carter in *The New York Times*. In fact, if you don't have purpose and aren't meaningful, that will lead to a shorter life. So, what do you want to do with your precious time ahead?

5. RELATIONSHIPS WILL CHANGE AND GROW

Committed, romantic relationships may face new challenges as we get older. We may have given them short shrift while we were working like mad, getting the kids to school and dealing with day-to-day life. I've had good friends divorce in their 60s. My mother and stepfather divorced at 74 and 90 years of age, respectively. A friend's wife died suddenly at age 70, and they'd planned to finish their lives together. Today, 18 months later after extensive counseling and hard internal work, he has built a new life and is dating.

"Having studied this age group's issues extensively, many have planned financially for retirement and yet they haven't considered what they want their relationship life to look like," notes my friend Norene Gonsiewski, MSW, LCSW, long-time marriage counselor and co-author of "Rock Solid Relationship." "It's apt to be daunting when they look at the few columns they have left and yet is the urgency ever greater? This age group has the highest growth in divorce. Family lawyers report that 25 percent of their divorcing clients are 65 years and older, and the highest affair rate is currently in this age group. Having a strong life plan could put zest back in your relationship."

That being said, I see a lot of 60+ people out in public being very affectionate and putting their arms around each other and holding hands—more than ever. But intimacy for some may have waned, or the relationship has become locked. Communication may need work, and it can be difficult to make each other a priority. You may also want to seek a therapist's help.

Exercises for People 60+

As you continue to reflect, these exercises will help you organize your thoughts about your future.

1. **Do a review of your first Two Acts of life: birth-29 and 30-59.** What happened? Where did you come from? What happened to you positively and negatively? What did you dream you'd do? What did you accomplish? Go back and look at family photos. Read old journals and letters. Look at your resumes. Think about the choices you made. Your regrets. Forks in the road and what might have happened had you taken the other path.

"PEOPLE ARE SO WORRIED ABOUT GETTING OLD. I NEVER THINK ABOUT IT. I THINK PEOPLE SHOULD JUST TAKE ADVANTAGE OF BEING ALIVE."

—**Iris Apfel**, *95-year-old fashion icon, businesswoman and interior designer in HBO's 2017 documentary "If You're Not in the Obit, Eat Breakfast"*

2. **What is your life's purpose now?** Why are you here now?

· What gives you happiness, a sense of accomplishment or satisfaction, or meaning and fulfillment? Is it enough?

· What are you missing?

· Who are you really?

· What are your values?

· What do you stand for?

· What do you want your identity to be at 60, 70, 80 and 90?

· What's upcoming that may add to your life's purpose?

....

....

....

....

....

....

....

....

3. **What haven't you accomplished?** What dreams do you have that are not yet actualized? Would you do something at 70 or 80 that would give you satisfaction, income and identity? Would you work three-quarters or half-time?

....

....

....

....

....

4. **If you have one, two or three decades left, what's most important to accomplish?** What are your top three vacation destinations? What's left undone in your life? What do you really, really want to get done?

....

....

....

....

....

....

....

5. **If you have children, will they have children?** Parents get a second go being grandparents, being present in a whole new way in terms of mindfulness and also being able to separate and recover. What do you wish you had done differently with your kids? Can you now do things differently with your adult children or your grandchildren?

....

....

....

....

6. **How are you going to keep learning and growing?** You may have gone to school for 20 years of your life (adding up elementary, middle and high school, community college, trade school, college). You now have 30 years ahead. How are you going to grow your brain and world?

....

....

....

....

....

7. If you're in a committed relationship, what do you want it to look like in the coming decades?

- How will you keep your relationship fresh?

- How will you ensure it actually is?

- Will you continue to have sex? How often? What changes to your sex life do you want to make or will you have to make?

- What will you do together and apart?

- Who has the reins to the finances? Is it fair/unfair? Do you make decisions together? Is there complete transparency? Are you considering gender differences in longevity in your financial planning?

....

....

....

....

....

....

....

....

....

8. **If you're single, do you like being single and want to remain so?** How might that change? What would you give up having a romantic partner?

....

....

....

....

....

....

9. **What changes do you need to put in place should you become incapacitated?**

....

....

....

....

....

10. **Should your partner (or support system) start to disintegrate—or die unexpectedly tomorrow—how will you manage your life?** What possibilities would you envision for your life? What changes might occur?

....

....

....

....

....

11. **How are you going to stay fresh?** How are you going to stay interesting? Do you actively listen (including to yourself)? How?

....

....

....

....

....

....

....

12. What other outside influences/scenarios might impact your life plan?

....

....

....

....

....

....

....

....

....

....

....

....

Step 2

Build Your Timeline

In Step 2 you'll get:

1. A timeline of your life

2. Your goals and dreams plotted by year

3. A visual plan you can hang on your hallway or office wall to keep you on track

"YOU'VE GOT TO HAVE A PASSION, A LOVE FOR WHAT
YOU'RE DOING, OR YOU SHOULDN'T BE DOING IT."

—**Gene Cernan,** *the last man on the moon*

The Power of Writing Things Down

It's amazing: The simple act of writing goals or desires down—putting pen to paper— makes things happen. As airy-fairy as this sounds, it truly opens things up in the universe, and the process I'll be taking you through to develop your Intentional Life Plan will put things in motion for you.

Henriette Anne Klauser, in her book "Write It Down, Make It Happen," notes the power of writing down your goals. Writing helps you clarify things—but there is also magic that happens when you write down your goals on a timeline.

Klauser describes this alchemy as "Go! Incidences"—signals and patterns that come to us—which Carl Jung called "synchronicities" and others call "messages from the universe." Some believe we send out energy waves, transmissions, and vibrations that attract people and solutions to us. Others call it "divine intervention." What these views have in common is a duality that puts us in charge, while also implying a higher power who is guiding, watching out, and caring about each and every one of us. Writing down our goals sends a notice to the universe that says, "Hey, I'm ready!" And Go! Incidences are messages coming back: "I got your signal, and I'm working on it."

Seventeen years ago, I climbed to the top of Washington's 3,000-foot Dog Mountain. As I sat there, looking over the Columbia River Gorge National Scenic Area, I thought, "We should live out here and buy a ranch." Soon after, Melinda and I developed our first Intentional Life Plan and wrote, "Buy a ranch in the Gorge." Within four years, we did, and we've been living on an 80-acre ranch overlooking the east side of Mount Hood ever since.

It works! Our planning process has helped us realize the life we dreamed. We quit our jobs and started a business. We travel to a different foreign country every other year. We're proactively helping our parents as they become older. And we have a financial plan we are working toward.

Klauser is right: Writing it down makes things happen.

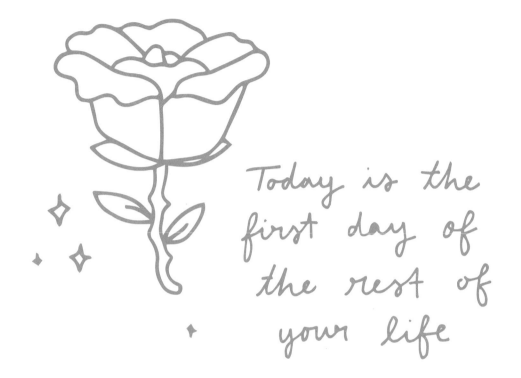

Today is the first day of the rest of your life

"Working on my plan in pairs was very helpful for me. I do think that is because I worked with one of my dearest friends, who knows me better than anyone. Uncovering your biggest dreams through this process can also expose some of your deepest fears, so my advice would be if you choose to bring a friend, bring a person with whom you have a high level of trust. Otherwise, insecurities may prevent you from making the most of this process."

—Foundation director

Get Ready for Your Intentional Life Planning Day

When I was a child, my parents had a gift shop, The Stuffed Squirrel, that sold posters, one of which was of a young girl extending flowers as a gift with the phrase, "Today is the first day of the rest of your life." Imagine how exciting and what a gift it is to plan your life ahead!

You've already set energy in the universe in motion by doing all the hard pre-work in Step 1. In this next step, you'll do the most important part of our process and spend a day being creative and spontaneous.

In this step, you'll create your Intentional Life Plan, and obtain a clear view of your road ahead and the goals you want to accomplish. Our workshop participants have told us they've appreciated coming out of this day with "something concrete instead of the vague goals I've had for myself." Rather than just saying you'll plan your life one day, you'll actually do it—you'll focus and build a visual format and a practical structure.

At Nike, we developed plans for everything. They often weren't long or complicated, but they included a lot of thinking and imagining, all driven by the Nike mission: "To bring innovation and inspiration to every athlete in the world." What did we want to get done? What were our objectives? What did we want to have happen as a result? What resources did we need to accomplish our goals? Who was going to do what and when? What was the timeline? How would we measure success? How were we furthering the company's mission?

My Nike colleague Mary Slayton underscored the value of a strategic plan: "A plan's not strategic," she told us, "unless it allows you to say 'no.'" That means setting priorities as to what matters most and staying focused.

"DON'T ASK YOURSELF WHAT THE WORLD NEEDS. ASK YOURSELF
WHAT MAKES YOU COME ALIVE, AND GO DO THAT, BECAUSE
WHAT THE WORLD NEEDS IS PEOPLE WHO HAVE COME ALIVE."

—Howard Thurman

Get Started

By setting priorities for your life, you, too, will be able to stay focused on what matters most. So, let's get going!

You may do this planning day by yourself, with a close friend, or with your spouse or partner. Make this day sacred: Schedule a Saturday or a Sunday—or a day you are on vacation— to create your plan. Set aside three to four hours at least. Don't multitask or look at your smartphone or computer screen this day. Don't answer your phone if it rings. This is about your life!

Create a comfortable space. You'll need a long counter or table, plus some stools or chairs. Prepare beforehand some refreshments and healthy snacks.

Plan to celebrate at the end of the day by going to a park, heading to a movie or play, or having a nice dinner.

1. PURCHASE YOUR SUPPLIES

You'll need the following:

· A six-foot-long sheet of butcher paper (one for individual planning or one for couples to share)

· Multicolored, small Sticky Notes (extra sticky, if you can find them; I like 1x3.5" ones; 3x3" is another option)

· Notepads

· Pens and pencils

· Markers (water-based, non-bleed)

· Blue painter's masking tape

· Scotch tape

· Ruler

· Your digging work—responses to questions and notes from Step 1

Spread your butcher paper out across the counter and tape it down so it stays flat.

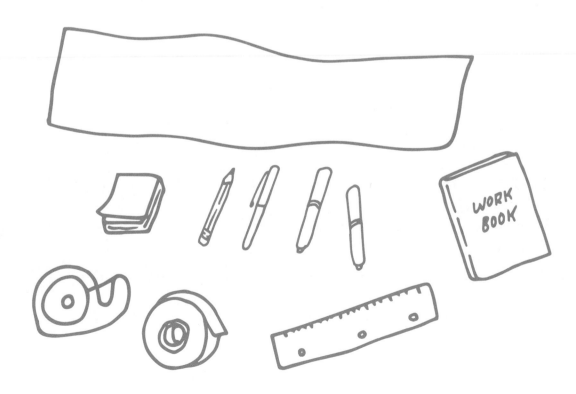

2. CALCULATE HOW LONG YOU WILL LIVE

If life is a project, and you only have so much time to complete it, how much time do you have? Let's find out.

Go online and use the excellent life calculator developed by University of Pennsylvania professors, which factors in age, gender and more: **myabaris.com/tools/life-expectancy-calculator-how-long-will-i-live.**

Another calculator you can use (figures in stress, sleep and habits, air quality): **livingto100.com.**

I probably will live until I am .... years old.

"YOU ARE YOUR
BEST THING."

—Toni Morrison

3. BUILD YOUR LIFE TIMELINE

Now that you know approximately how long you have to live, create a timeline.

At the top of your butcher paper, from left to right, title columns starting with the current year and add the years to your approximate end-of-life date.

Then draw in pencil or light ink a vertical line delineating each decade (10 years).

CURRENT YEAR	+1	+2	+3	+4	+5	+6	+7	+8	+9	XX	XX	XX	XX	XX	XX	XX	XX	XX	XX	XX	XX	XX

Stand back and look at how many decades you have ahead. What does it look like? What are you feeling/thinking?

4. ADD KEY DATES AND LIFE EVENTS

Add these key ages/dates and your initials just below the years at the top of
your timeline:

· Years you turn 20, 30, 40, 50, 60, 70, 80 and 90.

· Then add the years your partner, children, mom, dad, siblings, in-laws, grandparents,
etc., turn 20, 30, 40, 50, 60, 70, 80 and 90.

XX	XX	XX	XX	XX	XX	XX	XX	XX	XX		XX	XX	XX	XX	XX
	ME		WIFE	SON			DAD						MOM		
	50		50	21			80						80		

"I am goal-oriented, so this balanced all of my pie-in-the-sky thinking."
– IT technician

XX	XX	XX	XX	XX	XX	XX	XX	XX	XX	XX	XX	XX	XX	XX
	ME 50		WIFE 50	SON 21			DAD 80					MOM 80		
		EMPTY NEST		SON TO GRAD. COLLEGE								RETIRE		
				WEDDING ANNIV. 25 YEAR								PARENTS TO MOVE IN WITH US		
												GRAND CHILDREN?		

Add key family milestones:

- Birth of your future children
- Year your children start driving, graduate from high school/college
- Probable years your children will marry
- Probable years of grandchildren
- Anniversaries (work, relationship, close friends and family)
- Year child support ends (if divorced)
- When you become eligible for Social Security
- Year you expect your parents to die (you may want to live closer to them as they age)
- Expected retirement date

5. CREATE YOUR STICKY NOTES

Now, take all your ideas from Step 1 (pre-planning phase) and start generating Sticky Notes.

- Write one idea per individual Sticky Note that describes each goal you want in your life, including things you want to do solo, with a partner or spouse, with family members or with friends.

- Want to go to Thailand? Buy a house or new car? Learn guitar? Volunteer for Meals on Wheels? Quit your job? Save for college? Remodel your kitchen? Develop a financial plan? Write each goal down on a Sticky Note. Go for it! No editing right now. This is about imagining and getting it all out there!

- Melinda and I use one color for all our Sticky Notes; some workshop participants have used multiple colors to further define their planning areas.

- Revisit the detailed Intentional Life Planning areas in Step 1 and write more Sticky Notes as goals come to you.

6. ADD YOUR STICKY NOTES TO YOUR TIMELINE

Next, start sticking your goals and ideas onto your Intentional Life Plan butcher paper.

- What do you want or need to do this year? Next year? Future years?
- Put the higher-priority goals at the top of your plan, and lower priorities lower by year.

Step back and take stock:

- What's missing?
- Are there areas you didn't cover?
- How are your goals spread out?
- How many do you have for the year coming up? Is that a reasonable number?
- Are your highest priorities highest by year?
- What do you see overall? Any big themes? Anything that gets your heart skipping?

The joy of Sticky Notes is you can move them around. If you don't complete all of this year's goals, you can move them to next year or into the future. Or you can throw them away if your goals have changed.

You can have too many goals for a given year, so think about what's reasonable—say, 3 to 10 things this year you might do. (Hey, if you get them all done, you can add more!) The key here is to think about the major life goals you want to accomplish over the course of your life.

NOTE: If you're midlife or younger, you may see a lot of blank space at the right end of your Intentional Life Plan timeline. That's OK: We tend to know what our life goals might be in the next 10 to 20 years, but further out we may be less sure. Likewise, some older people may have a view of the next two years, but not beyond.

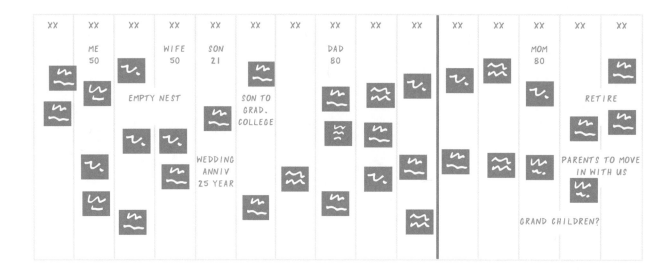

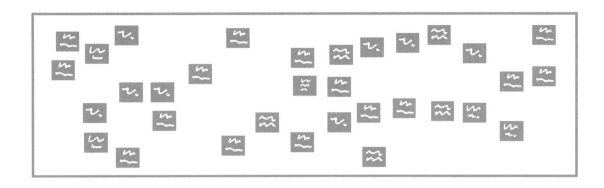

7. HANG YOUR TIMELINE SOMEPLACE YOU'LL LOOK AT IT OFTEN

Once you are satisfied with the timing of your goals, tape down the tops of your Sticky Notes (some Sticky Notes lose their grip and fall).

It's important to then hang your Intentional Life Plan someplace private and convenient for you so you'll have it to look at as you go about your day. The visual reminder of the plan and your life goals is incredibly powerful.

Be mindful where you hang your plan. For example, you may not want guests to see that you're quitting your job this year!

Our workshop participants have hung their life plans in stairways, guest rooms and home offices. Samantha and Jeff's is in their stairwell: "Our guests see it and ask us questions about it, reminding us and them about the plan. Just having it exposed was kind of extra." One workshop alumna is so serious about staying at it that she keeps hers in her bathroom. Another has hers in her bedroom "so it's the first thing I see every day. There are privacy pros and cons," she notes.

Melinda and I keep our plan in a hallway, and it was fun when our daughter's boyfriend visited and asked us about my goal to climb Mount Hood. Psychology professor and MacArthur Fellow Angela Duckworth, in her book "Grit: The Power of Passion and Perseverance," writes that the key to success isn't just talent, but also passion and persistence. "As much as talent counts, effort counts twice," she writes. I agree—but it all starts with a plan by which you can apply your passion and persistence!

I check off life goals we've accomplished throughout the year, which always feels good, and always leave them on the plan so we can go back in time and enjoy what we've accomplished.

We also each add Sticky Note ideas during the year when we discuss a possible life goal. We review those in our monthly check-ins and also in our yearly planning sessions.

You now have a large, flexible timeline full of goals that will be prioritized into an actionable plan in the next chapter.

"It was a huge revelation that our entire life plan was contingent on selling our business."

—Small business owner

"LIFE IS WHAT HAPPENS WHILE YOU ARE BUSY MAKING OTHER PLANS."

—Allen Saunders

Special Instructions for Couples in Step 2

Keep these ideas in mind as you put together your timeline:

- As individuals and as a couple, this is extremely intimate work, which can bring up all sorts of feelings—happiness, sadness, exhilaration, fear and risk. That's all OK.

- If need be, just get it all down on your joint timeline as two individuals, and then engage in conversation afterward when you've got all your Sticky Notes on your timeline, noting where your goals are solo, where they may conflict and where they may complement each other.

- Speak from the heart. Remember to breathe. Feel free to take breaks. Go for a walk. Hug and kiss.

- You each have equal parts in this. This should be a safe place for you each to speak. Speak using "I." Listen to each other. Be curious: ask and inquire ("Help me to understand ..."). One of you may be an introvert who needs time to think. Give your partner time. Everything is fair game. No blaming each other or assigning tasks to your partner. No editing. Try to capture everything.

- Don't judge; support each other. You don't have to own the other person's goals—some of them may not be yours. Never make your partner compromise a dream or goal because you don't agree with it or because it doesn't fit with your plan. Be supportive and create a way to make it work. Get it all out on the timeline.

- Some of the things you identify today you will want to do, and will do. Some of them you may do later, or not do at all. What's important is getting the process started and the ideas out there.

Turn Your Timeline Into an Actionable Plan

In Step 3 you'll get:

1. Greater clarity about your life goals for the coming year

2. A precise understanding of the steps needed to convert your life goals into actions

3. An easy-to-use action plan to turn your plan into reality

"A DREAM WRITTEN DOWN WITH A DATE BECOMES A
GOAL. A GOAL BROKEN DOWN INTO STEPS BECOMES
A PLAN. A PLAN BACKED BY ACTION MAKES YOUR
DREAMS COME TRUE."

—Greg Reid

Actualize Your Plan

Congratulations! Now you have an Intentional Life Plan and can see it on a timeline. In Step 3, you'll now turn your intentions into actions.

Back at Nike, we created "action plans" that included all the steps we needed to complete for the launch of a new product, assigning who was responsible along with deadlines. In the same way, to realize your big life goals, you'll next need to determine what concrete steps you need to take to make them real—and then assign owners and deadlines.

Goals can sometimes seem amorphous, lofty or hard to accomplish. Where do you even start? It's really important to break down your goals into action steps—starting with the 10 to 40 steps you will need to take to make them happen. One step leads to another, and so on.

Management gurus Peter Drucker and George Doran developed a SMART goal formula to help people evaluate their goals and refine vague or ill-defined goals into ones that can more easily be accomplished. Ideally you want your life goals to be:

- **S**pecific (is your goal well-defined?)
- **M**easurable (can you measure your progress toward the goal's completion?)
- **A**chievable (can you really achieve this goal?)
- **R**elevant (is it realistic and relevant?)
- **T**ime-bound (when are you going to accomplish this goal?)

Remember, the sheer act of writing your dreams and goals down, which you did in Step 2, and the visual power of looking at your life plan regularly have already set you on the path of realizing your life goals.

In Step 3, you'll now create a prioritized, actionable plan to realize your intentions—a plan you will immediately set to use from here on out.

One of our workshop alumna had the life goal to sing in public before an audience. She broke that life goal down into steps that included hiring a band, determining her set list, rehearsing, finding a venue and then inviting friends. I was proud to be in the jazz club audience when she took the stage for an hourlong set, and she credited Intentional Life Planning with helping her achieve her goal.

1. REALIZE YOUR GOALS

How do you go about turning your life goals into a concrete action plan?

Set reasonable expectations. Your life is busy enough as it is with daily duties. You have a lot going on—work, getting kids to and fro, taking care of loved ones and, frankly, stuff happens. Try to set reasonable expectations so you achieve what you've set out to accomplish.

Prioritize your life goals for the coming year. Focus on the milestone achievements that, when you look back in a year, will have made a difference in your life. How many goals are there? If you have more than 10 life goals for this year, that's probably too many. Move some to next year.

Make each of your life goals as realistic as possible. Having a big goal like "eating better" is one thing. But unless it's actionable, it may hang out there like one of those New Year's resolutions we never get to.

Continue to evaluate and sharpen your life goals using the SMART goal formula. Create the action steps you will need to achieve your life goals.

These were some of our workshop participants' life goals:

- · Paint/repair living room foyer
- · Sleep in treehouse
- · Take Korean class
- · Do one volunteer activity

2. CREATE AND CALENDARIZE YOUR ACTION STEPS

Consider what action steps you need to achieve each life goal.

What is your first step in moving toward your goal? Second step? Third? Who does what? When will you start? How much of the year will it take? Take your most important goal or intention, and break it down by steps and owner.

Now, put your action steps into a simple timeline, charting out what you want to get done by quarter. This is easy and uncomplicated—a short list of what you aim to do each quarter:

Q1: January, February, March
Q2: April, May, June
Q3: July, August, September
Q4: October, November, December

You may have a future life goal that may take years to accomplish. Break it down into action steps over the period of time you think will be needed, including the required steps this year by quarter. Here is an example of an action plan through Q3 complete with action steps broken down by quarter.

	REPAIR LIVING ROOM	SLEEP IN TREEHOUSE	TAKE KOREAN CLASS
When	Q1	Q2	Q3
1st Step (Who)	RESEARCH CONTRACTORS (EZRA) CLIP MAGAZINE ARTICLES; SEARCH PINTEREST FOR IDEAS (KATHY)	RESEARCH TREEHOUSE RENTALS (KATHY)	ASK FRIENDS FOR PROGRAM/CLASS REFERENCES (EZRA)
2nd Step (Who)	INTERVIEW CONTRACTORS; SEEK BIDS AND CHECK REFERENCES (E&K)	DISCUSS OPTIONS AND TIMING (E&K)	CONSIDER CLASS SCHEDULE AND COSTS (E)
3rd Step (Who)	SIGN CONTRACT; SCHEDULE WORK (E&K)	BOOK TREEHOUSE! (K)	SIGN UP FOR CLASS; MAKE PAYMENT (E)
4th Step (Who)	CHOOSE PAINT COLORS (E&K)	FIND/SCHEDULE CAT SITTER (E)	
5th Step (Who)	LINE UP CAT CARE, HOUSE SITTER, ETC. (K)		

Incorporate your Intentional Life Plan goals and action steps for the year into your daily/weekly planner, calendar or task list.

We keep just our life goals, but not our action plan, on our Intentional Life Plan timeline so we can see the 5 to 10 big things we want to accomplish this year.

To keep them in front of me and easy to find and review, I keep our yearly life goals other places I use to manage my life and tasks—my Things smartphone app and Evernote.

I've also incorporated them into the dashboard that I've created for my work tasks.

Others use Excel, Word and other applications to manage their quarterly life goal action steps. The goal is to make it simple and easy to look at your yearly life goals so they're never far from your mind. (See Resources section on page 108.)

"I did my show, which I have to say I don't think without the plan would have happened. There was something about that really hard commitment."

—Jazz club singer

On the next several pages, you'll find flexible templates you can use and copy to break your life goals into action steps. You can use one page for several life goals or for one life goal that may take more time than one quarter.

When	Q1	Q2	Q3	Q4
1st Step (Who)				
2nd Step (Who)				
3rd Step (Who)				
4th Step (Who)				
5th Step (Who)				

When	Q1	Q2	Q3	Q4
1st Step (Who)				
2nd Step (Who)				
3rd Step (Who)				
4th Step (Who)				
5th Step (Who)				

When	Q1	Q2	Q3	Q4
1st Step (Who)				
2nd Step (Who)				
3rd Step (Who)				
4th Step (Who)				
5th Step (Who)				

When	Q1	Q2	Q3	Q4
1st Step (Who)				
2nd Step (Who)				
3rd Step (Who)				
4th Step (Who)				
5th Step (Who)				

When	Q1	Q2	Q3	Q4
1st Step (Who)				
2nd Step (Who)				
3rd Step (Who)				
4th Step (Who)				
5th Step (Who)				

"THE FIRST STEP TOWARDS GETTING SOMEWHERE IS TO DECIDE THAT YOU ARE NOT GOING TO STAY WHERE YOU ARE."

—J.P. Morgan

Take That First Step

As you develop an action plan for each life goal, you may not know where to start. That's OK. A project may seem overwhelming before you begin, but don't over-complicate things at this stage.

But everything gets easier with that first step: Once you take it, you put things in motion, and the steps that follow suddenly become clearer.

Never developed a budget? Maybe start with research or by meeting with a financial planner. Or talk to a friend or ask your Facebook friends about the best approach.

Never remodeled a kitchen? Consider the layout, clip ideas from magazines, houzz.com and Pinterest, and go to a showroom to look at cabinets. Then create a sample budget, research and meet with contractors, and develop a project schedule. Whatever your goal, think through what the first, second and third steps might be.

And if you can't figure it out, ask for advice. The key is to break down each life goal into small, achievable steps so you can begin taking action.

"This gave me space to dream without limitations. Sometimes my more practical side can come in and shut down my 'outside the box' ideas for life. Putting these ideas down and exploring what it would take to make them happen made me realize that they are achievable."

—Writer

"Great to get all those rambling ideas out on paper. I liked not coming up with action steps for everything. Simple. It allows me to see what's important and create action steps independently."

—Corporate executive

"ENTHUSIASM IS COMMON.
ENDURANCE IS RARE."

—Angela Duckworth

Special Instructions for Couples in Step 3

Here are some additional ideas to consider as you create your plan with your partner:

· This can be a wonderful time to talk, imagine and have some fun. What one crazy thing would each of you want to do? Would one of you want to be a disco dancer? Put some play into it!

· Be equal in this: Discuss equally. Divide tasks equally.

· Don't assign without discussing. You are doing this in partnership. This is your life together!

· If one person is good at something, they should get that task. For example, if someone is better on the phone, perhaps they should be assigned to the phone calls.

· Use the "I" word, and don't blame or criticize your partner.

· Use reflective listening skills (detailed in the book "Getting the Love You Want" and using Imago Dialogue). Have one person be the Sender (speaker) and the other the Receiver (listener). The Sender speaks first. The Receiver listens and then mirrors back what they heard. Then the Receiver asks if they got it right. The Sender can then acknowledge what they got right and what the Receiver may have missed. The Receiver then empathizes (e.g., "That might have made me feel ...."). The process then reverses. More info: imagoworks.com/the-imago-dialogue/steps.

· How can you support each other's goals? What can you do to enable your partner's goals? Can their goals go first? It's crucial to support each other, compromise, and negotiate so you each can achieve your goals and wishes. If our relationship is about passionate friendship (and partnership), my goal is to help my wife achieve her goals, and vice versa (and it gives me great happiness to do so).

· After you're done, go do something nice together. Watch your favorite TV show together or toast each other. Plan on some affection and give each other a hug or a thumbs up. This has been really challenging, important work. Yay, team!

Step 4

Keep to the Plan

In Step 4 you'll get:

1. Advice for how to stay on plan

2. Guidance on updating your plan

3. Help for when you fall off track or don't accomplish your goals

> "I DON'T WANT TO GET TO THE END OF MY LIFE AND FIND THAT I HAVE JUST LIVED THE LENGTH OF IT. I WANT TO HAVE LIVED THE WIDTH OF IT AS WELL."
>
> —Diane Ackerman

Plan to Reality

Now that you have an Intentional Life Plan and have identified the action steps you need to realize your life's wishes, how do you stay on your plan and make sure it materializes?

You've already got tons of "to-dos" every day at home and work—it's called daily living. But those regular tasks and responsibilities can get in the way of accomplishing your life objectives. In addition to the day-to-day obligations, surprises and unexpected adversities can get in the way—such as divorce, cancer or the deaths of loved ones. That's life! What's key to this Intentional Life Planning process is having a strategic, linear plan and tactical formula to bring you back to your vision and help you focus on what's important to make it happen.

Our workshop co-facilitator, Mel Lee, advises: "I think life is a process. However, without having a life plan written down, it is easy to miss the cues and signals as to where we are in the process. Or even that it is happening. Your plan can be written in pencil, changed at any time, but without it, time passes quickly!"

At Nike, we had weekly project check-ins to review progress against our action plans. We coded our plans green (done), yellow (in progress) and red (stopped), and discussed our progress, issues and next steps. Doing so kept us on track.

Similarly, Step 4 gives you the tools you need to keep to your plan. I'll share with you what's worked for us, and what we've heard from workshop alumni.

1. STAY ON TOP OF YOUR PLAN

Here's how to manage and stick to your plan:

Hang your Intentional Life Plan someplace visible where you live. As mentioned earlier, it's important to display your plan someplace you pass frequently so you can continually evaluate how you're doing this year, as well as see what's coming up next year and in the next 5 to 10 years.

Warning: Do not roll up your timeline, store it in a closet and never look at it again! Truly, one of the best things about having this butcher paper plan is the visual nature of the tool. We humans are visual. If you read your Intentional Life Plan regularly, or even just notice it out of the corner of your eye, it will have a subconscious impact.

Melinda and I once tried typing up our Intentional Life Plan into an Excel document, but it didn't hold a quarter of the power of having the timeline displayed on the large butcher paper sheet. It's too easy to file something away or roll it up, put it in a closet and forget about it. Literally and figuratively, you need to keep your intentions in your line-of-sight.

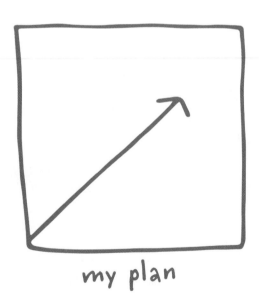

my plan

what actually happened

2. REVIEW YOUR LIFE GOALS AND ACTION STEPS EVERY MONTH

It only takes 10 minutes every month to review your plan, but make a date for yourself and stick to it!

Melinda and I love to make our plan check-ins fun and something to look forward to. We sometimes go out to breakfast and discuss our progress at a restaurant. You might take yourself out to lunch, or bring your yearly life goals into bed with you on a Sunday morning and review them. Friends working in pairs can schedule monthly check-in times and hold each other accountable. Our workshop alumnae Ashley and April touch base to let one another know when they have achieved a goal, and offer assistance to one another. Review your action steps every month. This is your life, and time's passing! It doesn't have to take long—even just five minutes—but be intentional.

Stay accountable and on task. Ask yourself as you review monthly:

· Am I on plan?

· What can I check off as done?

· If nothing has happened, or not enough, acknowledge that. Ask why. What's blocking me?

· What one to two steps can I commit to doing this month?

In our personal tracking of our progress, Melinda and I use red, green and yellow to code our quarterly action steps and yearly life goals to mark how we're progressing against them. Again, green means done, yellow means in progress but there may be a roadblock, red means no progress (stopped).

Also, consider sharing your life goals and action steps with friends and family. Sometimes great power can be derived from just talking out loud about what you aim to get done.

3. PRESERVE YOUR TIMELINE AND ADD NEW IDEAS

Photograph your timeline and keep the pictures stored somewhere safe and accessible. I always want to have access to our Intentional Life Plan from wherever I am. It's also helpful to have a backup just in case your butcher paper life plan gets damaged

Keep a list of new ideas to add to your plan as they cross your mind. I use Siri to dictate new ideas into my iPhone as they occur to me, then add them to our Intentional Life Plan for consideration. "Take Melinda to Cape Cod" struck me recently. I'll bring that up with Melinda at our next monthly check-in meeting, or create a Sticky Note and put it on the plan for future consideration.

4. RECALIBRATE YOUR PLAN YEARLY

Set aside a half-day each year to evaluate your Intentional Life Plan. New Year's Day or a day soon after the start of the year is a fun time to review the year that was, and to update your Intentional Life Plan for the coming year! It's an annual ritual in our household.

As you recalibrate, review your accomplishments for the past year and evaluate your life goals. Move or remove Sticky Notes that are no longer a priority or are no longer relevant. This is your life! Not going to France this year? Move the life goal years out. Never going to learn the ukulele? So be it. Take it off the timeline or put it on the bottom. Once you've evaluated your life goals, decide which ones you want to accomplish in the coming year, and develop a new action plan broken down into quarters for the annual life goals you want to accomplish.

5. CELEBRATE WHAT YOU'VE ACCOMPLISHED!

We human beings can be so critical, moving onto the next thing in life and in work without reflecting upon the progress we've made.

Take time to celebrate what you've accomplished as you review your plan every month and your yearly life goals. Put a checkmark or X on each Sticky Note as you accomplish a goal, and leave those accomplished Sticky Notes on your plan. It's amazing to go back and review your desired intentions and what you've already accomplished—and doing so will motivate you to stay on plan.

"BE IN LOVE WITH YOUR LIFE. EVERY MINUTE OF IT."

—Jack Kerouac

What to Do When You Fall off Track

Sometimes life really does get in the way, and we don't accomplish what we intended to get done this year or even for several years.

Every year I may have a life goal or two that I don't realize. This year, New York was a travel goal and I didn't get there. That's OK—I'll move that Sticky Note to next year. We had a lot going on.

That said, if you've had "take a class" as a goal for several years and have never gotten to it, perhaps it's time to remove that goal. Maybe it's no longer important. Or maybe it's something you might do in a future decade or when you're retired. If so, move the Sticky Note to later in your timeline, or put a big "X" over it if you want to keep it and remember you changed your mind and decided not to do it.

If something is really blocking you, journal about it. Or you may want to talk to a close friend or loved one, seek professional guidance from a therapist or a consultant, or take a class or join a group to help you get unstuck.

Marketer and author Seth Godin reminds us of the importance of not giving up: "Can you imagine how difficult the crossword puzzle would be if any given answer might be, 'There is no such word'? The reason puzzles work at all is that we know we should keep working on them until we figure them out. Giving up is not a valid strategy, because none-of-the-above is not a valid answer."

"What's possible?" Godin asks us to consider. "As soon as we stop denying the possible, we're able to focus our effort on making it happen."

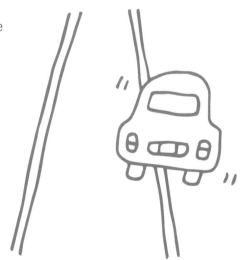

Special Instructions for Couples in Step 4

Remember these suggestions as you and your partner stick to your plan:

- Agree to meet monthly and put the meeting on your calendar and to-do list.

- Talk and discuss together constructively. Your job is not to ever be critical of your partner. Ask questions about how things are progressing or why they aren't.

- Remind yourselves that you may have some different life goals, and it is not your role to judge your partner's goals. It's your job to help your partner achieve their individual dreams and wishes.

- Be gentle with yourself and with your partner. You are lucky to have them and to have this life together. Laugh. Talk. Cry. Support.

- Commit and be accountable to each other. Haven't remodeled your utility room or started looking for that new job? Agree on what steps you both will take and when.

"DON'T JUST BE YOURSELF. BE ALL OF YOURSELVES. DON'T JUST LIVE. BE THAT OTHER THING CONNECTED TO DEATH. BE LIFE. LIVE ALL OF YOUR LIFE. UNDERSTAND IT, SEE IT, APPRECIATE IT. AND HAVE FUN."

—Joss Whedon

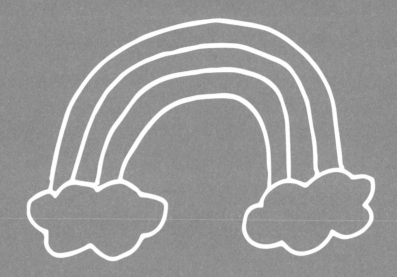

"REACH OUT. TAKE A CHANCE. GET HURT EVEN. BUT PLAY AS WELL AS YOU CAN. GO TEAM, GO! GIVE ME AN L. GIVE ME AN I. GIVE ME A V. GIVE ME AN E. L-I-V-E. LIVE! OTHERWISE, YOU GOT NOTHING TO TALK ABOUT IN THE LOCKER ROOM."

—Dame Marjorie "Maude" Chardin, *"Harold and Maude"*

Conclusion

Congratulations! You now have an Intentional Life Plan to guide your life.

By completing this workbook, you're well on your way to living your life with a capital "L." I hope this is the beginning of a fun, new journey for you, one that enables you to live with greater purpose and meaning—following your arrow, wherever it may lead you.

Stay focused—relentlessly—on your life goals. Be strategic. It's the big things that matter.

New ideas and goals will arise. That's OK. The key is to listen to your inner calling and actualize your dreams as they unfold.

Know, too, that small steps made consistently over time can lead to big change. Staying true to yourself and to your life's wishes is what this is all about.

While days can be full of repetition and we sometimes hit walls, always know there are endless opportunities to do things differently.

Life may be short, but you now have the tools to grab it by the horns. So, go ahead and live your life with intention, giving it everything you've got.

Resources

Couples Work/Imago Therapy

"Getting the Love You Want" by Dr. Harville Hendrix

imagorelationships.org, Imago Therapy and Workshops

"Rock Solid Relationship" by Norene Gonsiewski and Timothy Higdon

Life Planning

"The Artist's Way" by Julia Cameron

"Design the Life You Love" by Ayse Birsel

"Finding Your Own North Star" by Martha Beck

"The Fire Starter Sessions" by Danielle LaPorte

"Grit: The Power of Passion and Perseverance" by Angela Duckworth

"It's Never Too Late to Start Again" by Julia Cameron

"Letters to a Young Poet" by Rainer Maria Rilke

"Life Is a Verb" by Patti Digh

"The Life We Are Given" by George Leonard

"Where Will You Be Five Years From Today?" by Dan Zadra

"Wishcraft" by Barbara Sher

Teens

"It's Your Mind: OWN IT!" by Nicole Jon Sievers and Norene Gonsiewski

60s, 70s, 80s—Now What?

"How to Have a Good Day" by Caroline Webb

"Master Class on Aging" Aging Mastery program (10-course), ncoa.org/healthy-aging/aging-mastery-program/

"Prime Time" by Jane Fonda

"Rock Solid Relationship" by Norene Gonsiewski and Timothy Higdon

"Younger Next Year" by Chris Crowley and Henry S. Lodge, youngernextyear.com (sequel books as well)

Career Planning

"Are You a Corporate Refugee?" by Ruth Luban

"Do What You Are" by Paul D. Tieger and Barbara Barron-Tieger

"The Restless Soul in the Bathroom Mirror" by Lee Weinstein, nytimes.com

StrengthsFinder 2.0, strengths.gallup.com

Time Management

"Organizing from the Inside Out" by Julie Morgenstern

"Time Management from the Inside Out" by Julie Morgenstern

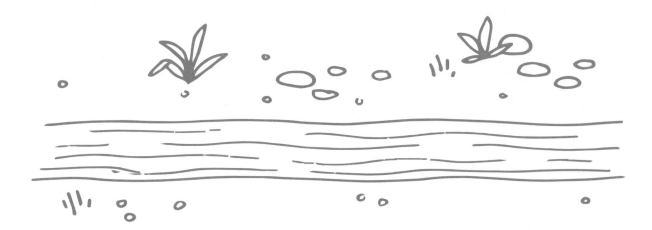

Life-Expectancy Calculators

deathcalendar.com (valuable calculator for its visual showing how many weeks you have lived, and how many you have left to live)

deathclock.com (light-hearted calculator showing your 'Personal Day of Death' and how many seconds left to live)

livingto100.com

myabaris.com/tools/life-expectancy-calculator-how-long-will-i-live (calculator developed by University of Pennsylvania professors factoring in age, race, gender, health and more)

Financial Planning

"Guide to Understanding Personal Finance" by Virginia B. Morris and Kenneth M. Morris

"No One Ever Told Us That" by John D. Spooner

"Smart Mom, Rich Mom" by Kimberly Palmer

End-of-Life/Family Caregiving

assets.aarp.org/www.aarp.org_/articles/foundation/aa66r2_care.pdf. A Planning Guide for Families

getyourshittogether.org (helps get your shit together one step at a time, starting with your will, living will/advance directive and life insurance)

The Gift of Caring" by Marcy Cottrell Houle and Elizabeth Eckstrom

theconversationproject.org

Apps/Tools

creativelive.com (curated creativity classes)

dailygreatness.com (journaling)

Evernote (shareable notes/to dos)

Google Keep (shareable notes/to dos)

Headspace (spirituality & meditation)

Insight Timer (spirituality & meditation)

mind-mapping.co.uk (mind mapping)

passionplanner.com (life planning)

Things (to-do list app)

Todoist (to-do list app)

Toodledo.com

Trello.com (productivity website and app)

wisdomheart.com (spirituality & meditation)

Workflowy (project management)

Wunderlist (shareable to-do list)

Accessories

"Remember You Will Die" wristwatch, mrjoneswatches.com/accurate

SPECIAL THANKS

Thanks to everyone who watched Melinda and my life planning in process and encouraged us to do workshops, and to Mel Lee for helping us develop this further. Mel (my mother) co-founded the 60s, 70s, 80s—Now What? workshops in Portland, and her wisdom in our discussions about retirement and aging greatly informed this workbook.

I'm very grateful for people who took time to give me their input: Puji Sherer, Ashley Henry, Norene Gonsiewski, Bob Applegate, Megan Armand, Maile O'Hara, Kate Fitzgerald, Lori McKenzie, April Severson, Gwenn Baldwin, Clark Binkley, Allison McGillivray, Amy Hunter, Vada Manager, Dana Pratt, Julie Beals, Matt Proctor, Jason Davis, Laurie Walker, Becky Brun, Samantha Irwin, and Emma and Sophie Weinstein.

Finally, I am forever thankful to Melinda, who helped closely on this book and has made my life infinitely happier since our meeting on the Nolan Ryan Patio in 1997. Let's stay together.